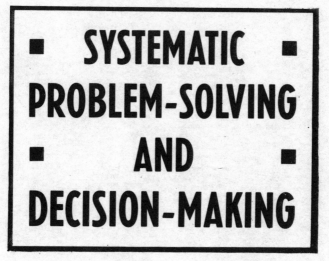

SYSTEMATIC PROBLEM-SOLVING AND DECISION-MAKING

Sandy Pokras

KOGAN
PAGE

First published in the United States of America in 1989 by Crisp Publications Inc, 95 First Street, Los Altos, California 94022, USA.

This edition first published in Great Britain in 1990 by Kogan Page Ltd, 120 Pentonville Road, London N1 9JN

British Library Cataloguing in Publication Data

A CIP catalogue record for this book is available from the British Library.

ISBN 0-7494-0159-1

Typeset by the Castlefield Press, Wellingborough, Northants.
Printed and bound in Great Britain by
Biddles Limited, Guildford

Contents

CHAPTER 1
Introduction

Have you heard the cliché, 'There are no problems, only opportunities'? This might sound like pie-in-the-sky optimism to anyone stuck in the middle of a difficult puzzle or a stressful people problem. But by using the proven, logical problem-solving and decision-making system presented in this book you can create opportunities from problems.

This book will show you how to confront problems rationally and systematically resolve crises. The decision-making method you learn will help you to break down touchy situations into component parts which can easily be dealt with individually. By using the comprehensive system presented, you'll know how to define, unravel, analyse, and solve difficult dilemmas and recurring foul-ups.

This book's primary emphasis is on communication in business, but the entire method presented here can be applied to personal situations as well.

The biggest problem-solving mistake is dealing with the symptoms of a problem rather than its root causes. Sometimes even the experts do not find the fundamental reason for the problem right away. When symptoms are treated, first-aid decisions are made. Then old symptoms reappear, or new ones emerge, and the same old problem returns.

By taking the six steps of systematic problem-solving and decision-making you can prevent problems from recurring. They are:

Step 1. Problem recognition
Step 2. Problem labelling
Step 3. Problem cause analysis
Step 4. Optional solutions
Step 5. Decision-making
Step 6. Action planning

The benefits and skills

What will be the advantages when you follow the step-by-step method presented above? Those who apply the techniques of systematic problem-solving and decision-making will receive the following benefits and learn the following skills:

- Definitions   You will learn to define accurately the real problem to avoid solving symptoms.
- Solutions   You can implement once and for all solutions instead of temporary expedients.
- Decisions   The decisions you make will be good decisions that can be implemented and will hold.
- Meetings   Your meetings will reflect productive problem-solving and decision-making.
- Buy-in   You will learn to obtain commitment from conflicting viewpoints to help define problems, reach decisions, clarify solutions and implement action plans.
- Teamwork   You will enjoy effective teamwork between differing individuals and groups while solving problems.

Your expectations
To get the most out of this book, you need to relate what you read to your personal situation. Answering the following questions can help you to concentrate on your typical problems and decision situations.

Personal expectations work sheet
Write your answers below.

> What problem situations would you like to correct?
>
>
>
> What difficult decisions do you need to work through logically?
>
>
>
> Which recurring problems and decisions would you like to resolve once and for all?
>
>
>
> Which of your problem-solving and decision-making skills would you like to improve?

Select a specific situation from the above to use as your Personal Case Problem while working through this book.

> As you work through this book, refer back to this work sheet. Experience has shown that this is the best way to learn a self-development method like this.

Your objectives

Rate your interest in the following objectives.

Objectives rating

I want to:

	Top priority	Interested	Some interest	Little interest
1. understand the *steps* of this problem-solving system.	☐	☐	☐	☐
2. know how to use the analytical *techniques* in each step.	☐	☐	☐	☐
3. recognise the vital role *communication* plays at each step.	☐	☐	☐	☐
4. know what *questions* to ask in order to stimulate communication at each step.	☐	☐	☐	☐
5. understand the *anatomy* of problems and why they persist.	☐	☐	☐	☐
6. understand how to confront problems to *prevent future stress*.	☐	☐	☐	☐
7. know how to distinguish between the *causes and effects* of problems.	☐	☐	☐	☐
8. know how to *label* a problem to facilitate discussion and analysis.	☐	☐	☐	☐
9. know how to find a problem's *root cause*.	☐	☐	☐	☐
10. know how to brainstorm optional *solutions*.	☐	☐	☐	☐
11. know how to evaluate optional solutions to *decide* on the most workable strategy.	☐	☐	☐	☐

	Top priority	Interested	Some interest	Little interest
12. understand the importance *action planning* to implement the chosen solution.	☐	☐	☐	☐
13. know how to *apply* the system to real-life problems as they occur in the future.	☐	☐	☐	☐

CHAPTER 2
Process Overview

What is a problem?

What does the term *problem* mean? Since the word is used so often in this book, you need a crystal-clear understanding of it. What do *you* think 'problem' means? Write your immediate thoughts below:

Your definition of the term *'problem'*:

Problem characteristics

The following checklist summarises the characteristic of problems. Items on this list always seem to be true about problems. It might be said that if these items exist your situation qualifies as a true problem. Tick off which of these characteristics apply to the cases you identified on the *Personal expectations work sheet* on page 9.

Problem characteristics checklist

Characteristics	These apply to my situations
Incomplete communication. Conversations have broken down or haven't even been started so that full understanding is lacking.	☐
Unknowns. Information is missing.	☐
Inaccurate information. Some of the known information is wrong.	☐
Confusion. People involved find themselves in a mental fog, stressed or overwhelmed by stimuli and choices.	☐
Hidden emotions. Feelings tend to emerge as you examine the situation.	☐
Different viewpoints. You and others have conflicting ideas.	☐
Changing impressions. As you investigate the situation, ideas, feelings and explanations change, sometimes radically.	☐
Balanced dilemma. A tug of war exists where no one person or idea is able to win.	☐
Persistence. The situation won't disappear.	☐

Problem anatomy

A problem is basically a dilemma with no apparent way out: an undesirable situation without a solution or a question that you can't currently answer. It's not just that things are different from the way you'd ideally like them to be – it's that you can't *fix* them no matter what you do. It's not simply a question that you haven't yet answered, it's one you can't explain. And it's a conflict or crisis that keeps coming back no matter what you do about it.

The anatomy of a problem boils down to this simple picture:

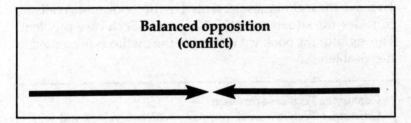

In words, a problem is an:

Idea ⟶	opposed by a ⟵	**Counter-idea;** or a
Force ⟶	opposed by a ⟵	**Counter-force;** or a
Goal ⟶	opposed by a ⟵	**Counter-goal.**

This table could go on but I'm sure you get the idea. For example:

You want to go shopping . . . *but* . . . you also want to save money.

You have to work with JR . . . *but* . . . you can't stand the person.

Your department thinks . . . *but* . . . your quality inspector wants
everything is working well   some changes.

The balanced opposition of situations is what generates the stress and confusion. The balance makes the problem persist. If one side becomes stronger and wins the struggle, the problem disappears. For example, your boss comes into the picture and decides how to handle things and everyone goes along with the decision. Hey presto, no more indecision. (Of course, if the underlying forces aren't resolved by this arbitrary choice, the problem will reappear.)

Case problem

To make the techniques presented in this book more realistic, consider the situation in the Consumer Tech case problem. Throughout the book we will apply the methods presented to this problem.

Consumer Tech case problem

Consumer Tech is a small company which develops and sells consumer products based on new technology. They have an extremely successful product, the Automatic Toothbrush. Recently, the Engineering Department came up with a dramatic new improvement. They've perfected a hands-free circuit which allows the brush to brush teeth electronically. Its called the Electronic Toothbrush.

This has created a problem. The Engineering Manager wants to introduce the new development right away. Unfortunately, during test production runs, the Manufacturing Manager has encountered problems in producing the new components. The Quality Manager is helping to determine what's causing the problems.

The Marketing Manager wants to announce the improvements immediately, but the Finance Manager is worried about making the large stock of Automatic Toothbrushes obsolete if the introduction is made too quickly.

Formal meetings about the Electronic Toothbrush, led by the company chairman, quickly deteriorate into heated arguments which lead nowhere. And impromptu meetings by the coffee machine often become shouting matches.

Looking at the *Problem characteristics checklist* on page 14, you will find all the problem characteristics present in this situation. Consumer Tech has tried to find a solution, but things are not progressing. It's becoming increasingly clear that some balanced opposition exists that no one has yet recognised. Unless this conflict is uncovered and resolved, things will probably go from bad to worse.

Case problem – your response

If you wanted to help, what would you do? Write your thoughts below. Feel free to refer to anything you have read thus far in this book. Later, after you have completed the book, reread this page to see how your suggestions have changed.

I would help Consumer Tech by:

Problem-solving methodology

The ideal method of resolving problems and making difficult decision involves two steps. This magic formula is guaranteed to work: in fact, it's never failed when applied correctly. Here it is:

1. Define the problem.
2. Decide how to solve it.

You already knew that, right? Although it seems obvious, most problem-solvers and decision-makers don't do a very good job of Phase 1, Problem definition. Instead, they rush off to Phase 2, Solution decision. Unless you define the problem thoroughly and accurately, your solution may not address what's really wrong underneath. In fact, most students of this system report that finding solutions is relatively easy. The difficulty is knowing exactly what to analyse and resolve.

How do you define a problem? And how do you find the best solution? Take a look at the *Problem-solving/decision-making outline* presented on page 19. This summarises the process, and will be referred to as the PS/DM outline throughout the book. Let's see how it works.

Problem-solving/decision-making outline

Each step below has a specific result. Only when you reach that result should you go on to the next step. For the best results don't skip *any* step.

Problem definition process	Result
1. **Recognition** Discuss and document individual views, proven facts, and relevant symptoms, until everyone involved accepts that there is a problem.	**Agreement that an issue needs resolution.**
2. **Label** Clearly document both sides of the exact conflict you want to resolve.	**An agreed statement of the problem.**
3. **Analysis** Find and agree on the *single* most fundamental source of the problem.	**Unanimous identification of the root cause which needs correcting.**
Solution decision-making process	**Result**
4. **Options** List *all* alternative strategies that have the slightest chance of resolving the problem and its root cause.	**A complete list of possible solutions.**
5. **Evaluation** Choose the best solution on your list by objectively evaluating the optional strategies.	**A firm joint decision on the chosen solution.**
6. **Action plan** Organise systematic steps of tasks, timing, staff, and resources to implement the decision in the real world.	**A complete step-by-step road map to translate the decision into reality.**

Each step of this outline will be discussed in detail throughout the rest of this book. Before going into each step in detail, it helps to have some guidelines to follow while applying the PS/DM outline. The *Overview checklist* presented on page 20 sums up the best way to approach any problem/decision situation.

Overview checklist

Review the checklist below to evaluate how well you currently deal with problems and decisions. You can refer back to it whenever you want to check your status.

Process overview checklist

Tick off those things you do now when making a decision or solving a problem:

I plan an agenda directed to a specific result.	_____
I stay on track and follow the agenda I've planned.	_____
I set and keep to ground rules for participation.	_____
I break down big problems into 'bite-sized' chunks.	_____
I complete each step before moving to the next.	_____
I return to the previous step if progress is bogged down.	_____
I know which technique I'm using at each point.	_____
I trust the process and keep to it as long as it works.	_____
I don't mix methods from different processes.	_____
I include all people or units affected.	_____
I openly consider divergent ideas as valuable input.	_____
I accept and integrate all views and feelings.	_____
I write down all thoughts, suggestions, and input.	_____
I keep a public running record of group discussion.	_____
I keep all material visible to all group members.	_____
I know which questions to ask at each step.	_____
I draw out complete answers from all present.	_____
I discipline myself to listen and respond.	_____
I assign distinct roles in the meeting.	_____
I stimulate the group's synergy and creativity.	_____
I seek agreement between divergent positions.	_____

CHAPTER 3
Communication Dynamics

Before starting the six-step process outlined on page 19, do you know what determines whether a problem-solver or decision-maker can make the process work? If you answered communication skills, you are right.

Poor communication causes barriers to solutions, while good communication skills are strong catalysts for problem-solving. Poor communication indicates the existence of a problem and may, in fact, be the cause of the trouble.

This chapter presents some critical mechanics to make communication work during the problem-solving and decision-making process.

How to get agreement on problems

Without mutual agreement that a problem exists, it can't be discussed, analysed or solved effectively. Good problem-solvers and decision-makers achieve agreement by applying this vital awareness; other views must be sought, respected and accepted. Communication is the process to make all this work.

The table below summarises guidelines for making the logical process work with human beings who sometimes aren't so logical and defines how to implement each guideline.

Guideline	How to apply it
If you feel you have a problem with someone or something, then there **definitely is** a problem.	Don't ignore it or let yourself be talked out of it. Probe for the other's awareness of the problem.
If a problem exists, everyone is **aware** of it in some way. Remember that your **awareness** of a problem may be quite different from others'.	To find out another's awareness of a problem, ask how things are different from the way they should be, or simply ask what their awareness of the problem is.
Find an accepted or observable fact as a **reference** point to start with.	Use production statistics, specific events, confirmed facts, something the other person has said, but *no* value judgements.
Find where **views** overlap.	Analyse the information you receive from everyone and see what the common points are.
Ask before you dictate.	State the general area you want to talk about, but immediately ask for the other person's feelings, thoughts, or observations
Solicit the other person's **point of view**.	Don't force your viewpoint on them, but show empathy for their position until they accept yours.
Avoid a **threatening**, accusatory climate.	Don't use leading or judge-mental questions ('Are you still screwing things up?') or lectures that elicit guilt or impose value judgements.
Create a strong and open working **relationship**.	If you're confronted with severe defensiveness or intimidation, use a less threatening approach.
Discover the falsehoods and **unknowns** that are causing the problem to persist.	Keep communicating until you find them.

What makes meetings work?

Let's apply the guidelines to meetings. Think back to several recent group problem-solving or decision-making situations you were involved in. What made the meetings work and what got in the way?

To answer this question, use the following *Force-field analysis* work sheet: *Positive/negative forces for meetings*. You will find this format several times later in this book. Two columns are headed by opposing brainstorming questions, in this case dealing with meetings. The question on the left asks for positive forces and the question on the right asks for negative forces. By playing a plus against a minus, your thinking loosens up and differences stand out more clearly.

When you fill in this form, don't use general terms such as 'communication' but specific descriptions: 'John wasn't prepared' and 'Jerry knew what questions to ask.'

FORCE-FIELD ANALYSIS WORK SHEET

Positive/negative forces for meetings

What makes meetings productive and effective?	What makes meetings unproductive and ineffective?

Meeting roles

Experts find that meetings work best when roles are well-defined. The meeting roles chart below explains how to separate responsibilities for meeting participants. The *Discussion leader* and the *Recorder* or *note-taker* are neutral. Everyone should be either a *Participant* or a *Presenter*.

Those present can wear different hats. Keeping roles separate is critical.

The most significant factor, the *Authority figure* of the group (ie the boss), must relinquish roles to meeting participants. If the authority figure doesn't do this, contributors will hold back, edit what they say, or challenge authority. An effective meeting will produce an open climate, a free exchange, and creative thinking without undue concern about the boss's reaction. This is hard to achieve, but defining roles will help.

Discussion leader
Directs the traffic of the discussion: announces each topic and its time frame, calls for input, asks stimulating questions, balances participation, reminds wanderers of the issue, and summarises at the end. Remains neutral and doesn't pass judgement without permission from the group.

Recorder
Keeps an accurate, public running record of what is said. Writes key words clearly on a flip chart or blackboard so that speakers feel they were heard correctly. Doesn't try to document everything but just gets the main points down.

Presenter
Presents outside information and major viewpoints in a systematic fashion. Articulates the position, gives supporting evidence, involves listeners, leads their thought process, and responds to questions.

Participant
Speaks his or her mind fully and clearly, listens intently, and absorbs what others have to say.

Authority figure
Ideally, the senior manager of the group should play an equal role in creative meetings. Since this is difficult in practice, it is recommended that the authority figure only assume the role of 'special participant', the one with the final say. Since the bosses are expected to be decisive, making one the discussion leader (who is supposed to be neutral), usually distorts a free and open exchange.

The discussion leader

The most challenging role is that of *Discussion leader* who directs the participation, but doesn't evaluate what is said.
   Controlling a dialogue has three phases:

- *Starting.* Getting individual or group discussions going
- *Guiding.* Steering the dialogue once started
- *Stopping.* Summarising, concluding or getting people to stop when they've already finished.

These sub-skills are detailed in the following checklist. Use this checklist to assess the effectiveness of a discussion leader and to identify those sub-skills needing development.

DISCUSSION LEADER SKILLS CHECKLIST

Starting skills

Know the issues before beginning. _____

Have easy reference notes and outlines available. _____

Get attention and call people to order. _____

Announce agenda items. _____

State points and problems clearly. _____

Establish realistic time frames. _____

Ask questions to get the group thinking. _____

Call all people by name. _____

Draw people out, especially quiet ones. _____

Notice and call on those with something to say. _____

Introduce new viewpoints into a continuing
discussion. _____

Guiding Skills

Listen carefully to all participants. _____

Use silence effectively and wait out pauses. _____

Read indicators and body language. _____

Remain neutral to ensure acceptance of all ideas. _____

Be sensitive and adjust to moods to keep things
moving. _____

Follow the agenda and keep discussions on track. _____

Restate topic so the group concentrates on one issue
at a time. _____

Steer discussions towards the desired results. _____

Clarify meanings and restate questions. _____

Avoid interfering with interactions. _____

Turn provocative questions back to the group. _____

Balance participation between different styles. _____

Mediate conflicting views so all are heard. _____

Manage diversions, digressions and distractions. _____

Watch the clock and keep time frames apparent. _____

Reflect on repeating patterns and ask for reaction. _____

Stopping skills

Acknowledge what people have said. _____

Ensure that each participant has a chance to finish. _____

Prevent individuals from talking at the wrong time. _____

Stop people who say things over and over again. _____

Protect individuals by discouraging attackers. _____

Let long-winded dominators know they've been
heard. _____

Check that questioners receive satisfactory
answers. _____

Announce when time deadlines are approaching. _____

Summarise what has been accomplished. _____

Know when to recap by listening for common
themes. _____

Show consensus by noticing and announcing it. _____

Ask for decisions and suggest conclusions. _____

Documentation during meetings

Effective problem-solvers and decision-makers keep accurate, up-to-date, legible notes. In group settings, this trait is especially important. The real rewards of good paperwork habits comes during later phases of the PS/DM outline.

Because of the confusion factor, especially at the beginning of a problem-solving situation, all sorts of information will be mixed together. Why go over this again later? If you carefully document items *as you go along*, you'll come to a decision sooner than those who do a poor job of recording the process.

Benefits of documentation

The following statements are benefits of clear documentation:

- Provides clearer, more accurate communication   _____
- Formally acknowledges individual contributions   _____
- Remembers and saves information for future use   _____
- Provides a fixed reference point for later use   _____
- Provides a record for all time   _____
- Allows outsiders to familiarise themselves with the situation   _____
- Shows evidence of the analysis process used   _____
- Encourages equal participation in a group   _____

Helpful techniques for documentation

The following techniques may help to make your documentation easier. Tick off any you plan to use:

Tape pages or flip chart sheets on walls or windows and keep notes on them.   ☐

Record what is said and decided on flip charts.   ☐

Use brief statements and short words that convey the meaning.   ☐

Have members of the group draft documents in rotation.   ☐

Tape record brainstorming meetings and have transcriptions made.   ☐

Have a reliable shorthand writer present to take notes.   ☐

Evaluate your next meeting

The next time you're in an interactive meeting, try this experiment to highlight the individual roles. Afterwards, have each member answer the questionnaire below. Then discuss each participant's reactions with the group. The objective is to discover how communication works best in this setting. Either you will find that each individual has naturally gravitated towards a specific role, or you need to define your meeting responsibilities better.

GROUP PROBLEM-SOLVING QUESTIONNAIRE

1. How was the agenda chosen?
2. Who led the discussion? Why?
3. Did you record issues presented?
4. Did all attenders participate? If no, why not?
5. Was a consensus reached? If no, why not?

Next time you are part of a problem-solving or decision-making meeting complete the following form to help you identify the points that were well handled and those that could be improved.

MEETING EVALUATION FORM

Criteria	0 to 10 rating (10 = High)
Preparation	
1. Participants informed in advance.	_____
2. Participants fully prepared for their role and contribution.	_____
3. Participants committed to dealing with common issues.	_____
4. Comfortable, uninterrupted, set-up room.	_____
5. Started on time.	_____
6. Clear well-presented agenda.	_____
Organisation	
7. Agenda followed efficiently with flexibility.	_____
8. Concentrated on one issue at a time.	_____
9. All views of each issue full considered before moving on.	_____
10. Smooth dialogue occurred through coordinated interchange of speaking and listening roles.	_____
11. Good pace maintained reflecting group momentum.	_____
Participation	
12. Participants actively contributed to a balanced interchange.	_____
13. Participants clearly presented their genuine ideas and feelings.	_____
14. Participants listened attentively to others' contributions.	_____
15. Participants responded directly and constructively to others' input.	_____
16. Spontaneous combustion of creative energy and thought stimulated full disclosure.	_____

Criteria	0 to 10 rating (10 = High)
Climate	
17. Spirit and emotional level of group was high.	_____
18. Discussion dealt with issues and their solution, not personalities and their conflicts.	_____
19. Individuals accepted others' views without personal attack or non-verbal put-downs.	_____
20. Members supported the leader and recorder as they guided the group.	_____
21. Disruptions and interruptions were smoothly disposed of.	_____
Closure	
22. Final judgements suspended until all input tapped.	_____
23. Succinct summaries recapped progress and acknowledged results.	_____
24. Discussion steered effectively to consensus and then stopped.	_____
25. Action items clearly announced and documented.	_____
26. Follow-up monitoring mechanism established.	_____
27. Meeting ended on positive feeling and mutual understanding.	_____

Six steps to problem-solving and decision-making

The next six chapters cover a systematic methods of problem-solving and decision-making. The six steps you will cover are:

1. Recognising the problem
2. Labelling the problem
3. Analysing the cause of the problem
4. Exploring optional solutions to the problem
5. Making a decision to solve the problem
6. Creating and following an action plan to resolve the problem

CHAPTER 4
Step 1: Problem Recognition

Problem-solving and decision-making begin by recognising that a situation needs resolution. Sometimes a problem gradually builds up without being noticed until it surprises you. Even when the trouble is obvious, it is a good idea to start with Step 1.

Problem recognition examines the 'tip of the iceberg'.

The Iceberg or 80/20 Rule
No matter how large the tip of an iceberg seems, 80 per cent of it lies below the surface of the water.

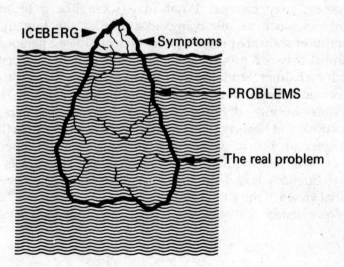

It is the same way with problems. No matter how serious or stressful the first encounter with a problem may seem, it is only a symptom of the underlying trouble or real problem.

Symptoms may be trivial, like one minor defect, or they may be serious issues that must be dealt with quickly, such as falling production levels. Either way, they are simply side effects of the real problem that lies beneath the surface.

The Iceberg Rule reminds you to have *patience*. You must understand the whole problem before rushing off to solve it. So examining, researching, investigating, tabulating and studying are the watchwords of Step 1.

Opening discussion – a good place to start

Problem recognition often starts with a discussion to gather symptoms from those involved. An iceberg may look different when viewed from different angles. Open-minded listening and genuine empathy are required to assess other viewpoints objectively. The objective is to get as much related information as possible on the table.

During an opening discussion your impressions of the problem may change. What may seem like a technical problem (such as not being able to find the bug in the computer software program) may turn out to be a personality conflict between programmers who don't share information with each other. Studying the human factors (soft symptoms) involved is important for understanding the problem. These include: feelings, divergent opinions, frustrations, personal reactions and hearsay. These are not hard scientific data (hard symptoms), but valuable nonetheless. During the opening discussion you should discover all the problem's effects and consequences, both hard and soft symptoms, and uncover all initial views of the situation.

Once listed it's helpful to categorise views as *hard* or *soft*.

Hard data	Soft data
Facts, results, events, history, statistics, forces, goals, procedures, physical phenomena, observable deviations, time factors, trends, productivity, quality and performance levels.	Feelings, opinions, human factors, friction, attitudes, satisfaction levels, stresses, frustrations, personality conflicts, behaviour, hearsay, intuition, 'gut' reactions, mental blocks.

How much is too much?

How far do you take problem recognition? You could say that getting all the facts (hard) and feelings (soft) is your target. The trouble is to know when you've discovered them all. (Actually, you will continue collecting facts and uncovering impressions throughout all the steps of the PS/DM process.)

A general indication that you've completed Step 1 is when everyone agrees that a problem needs resolution, and when all initial perceptions have been heard, listed and categorised.

Problem recognition techniques

There are four techniques in Step 1 that will help you to recognise a problem:

1. Symptom identification
2. Research methods
3. Data collection interviews
4. Group brainstorming

Certain techniques may be more appropriate in some cases than others. Watch for the need to vent frustrations. Problems and decisions are stressful and the people involved may need to release their emotional reactions. Venting is not always fun for the listener. However, when the air is cleared, people often become more rational and cooperative.

Each technique will be examined individually.

Symptom identification

The *Symptom list* is a simple form used to tabulate all visible manifestations, consequences, and effects. It is compiled by discussing and listing the initial data and perceptions of everyone involved.

Following is an example of a symptom list filled in with some of the facts from the Consumer Tech case problem on page 16.

Symptom	Hard	Soft
Current product selling well	√	
New product dramatic new improvement	√	
Engineering wants to make change now		√
Production department has component problems	√	
Poor quality probably based on test results	√	
Marketing Manager ready to announce new product		√
Finance Manager worried because stock levels high		√
Meetings lead nowhere		√
Heated arguments		√

Search for both hard and soft data. They're not always distributed 50–50, but you must examine both sides.

The following may be used for your Personal Case Problem.

SYMPTOM LIST

Symptom	Hard	Soft

Research methods

The data collection process will help you to study the background and effect of the problem systematically. This ten-step method leads you through designing and conducting an investigation of the problem. The *Data collection work sheet* on page 37 includes a series of methods you may choose for your study. A sheet outlining *Sample target data* is shown on page 38.

Data collection process

1. Identify the overall kind of information needed to define the problem (use the *Data collection work sheet*, page 37).
2. Select the data collection methods best suited for this type of information.
3. Define the specific target data you hope to collect with each appropriate technique (see *Sample target data*, page 38).
4. Collect the data required.
5. Analyse the data for patterns.
6. Establish a method to confirm the analysis, such as an experiment or more focused data collection process.
7. Collect data to confirm the pattern.
8. Document data and analysis in understandable form.
9. Prepare a visually orientated presentation if others need to use your analysis.
10. Present your data and analysis.

To be successful, first identify what target data you're after, and then design your research to concentrate on that area.

DATA COLLECTION WORK SHEET

General information needed to define the problem

Data collection method	Specific target data
Survey questionnaires One-to-one interviews Production statistics Quality statistics Financial statistics Work sampling Technical experiments Time/Motion studies Check sheets Focus groups Other:	

SAMPLE TARGET DATA

Results	Production levels	____
	Quality levels	____
	Error and rework levels	____
	Customer satisfaction	____
	Performance against target	____
	Expenditure versus budget	____
	Profit margin	____
	Return on investment	____
Resources	Personnel and training	____
	Time	____
	Capital	____
	Production capacity	____
	Physical space	____
	Equipment	____
	Stock	____
Organisation	Structure and function	____
	Roles and responsibilities	____
	Personnel policies and procedures	____
	Management performance	____
	Strategic planning system	____
	Organisational communication system	____
	Management information reporting system	____
	Management style and corporate culture	____
	Staff morale	____
External environment	Other departments	____
	Suppliers	____
	Labour	____
	Economy/industry	____
	New technology	____
	Market-place	____
	Job market	____
	Educational institutions	____
	Political	____
	Competitors	____
	Public goodwill	____

Obligations		
	Stockholders	___
	Contractual agreements	___
	Legal restrictions	___
	Labour contracts and employment law	___
	Government regulations	___
	Environmental considerations	___
	Social responsibility	___
	Financial commitments	___
	Employee health and welfare	___

Data collection interviews

Typically, the individual or group that starts the PS/DM outline in motion doesn't have all the related data. The research process can become extensive. Many problem-solvers and decision-makers use one-to-one interviews or group meetings as an initial data-gathering tool.

Data collection interviews are results-orientated, discussions specifically designed to understand an individual's view of the problem. The interviewer poses questions, listens and takes notes, but does not talk much. It is critical to know what needs to be asked before the interview.

The checklist on page 40 suggests some appropriate queries. This list can be used as a data collection planning aid. When trying to discover a problem that someone hasn't been completely open about or dealing with a group that doesn't really understand the situation, tick off those questions that you think will get you the information you need.

One word of caution: interviews can be inefficient or unproductive unless carefully structured in advance. Individual meetings are time-consuming, and voluminous notes take time to analyse. However, face-to-face meetings generate the most reliable information so they need to be seriously considered.

QUESTIONS TO UNCOVER PROBLEMS

Tick off those you plan to use during your case problem:

How are things going?

What problems have you had lately? _____

You seem troubled/upset/worried lately. What's happening? _____

What do you feel has been different around here lately? _____

What do you think changed? _____

How has your work been going? _____

Where do you need help? _____

What are you satisfied or dissatisfied about? _____

What do you find confusing? _____

What is your position on this matter? _____

What's on your mind? _____

Lately I've noticed some indications of lateness/slower work/ _____
lower quality. What do you think?

You don't seem yourself these days. What's the matter? _____

What are your feelings about this conflict/situation? _____

What opinions do you have about this problem? _____

What tensions/problems/disagreements/misunderstandings/ _____
conflicts/troubles have you been aware of lately?

What is your evaluation of this situation? _____

How closely do you think we've been seeing eye to eye lately? _____

Where do you think our views differ? _____

What have I done that you disagree with/object to/dislike/ _____
disapprove of/not understand/are confused about?

What about your viewpoint/attitude do you feel I've missed? _____

What do you think are our chances of success on this _____
programme?

What ideas and suggestions do you have regarding this _____
project?

In what areas do you feel confident/a lack of confidence? _____

What's bothering you? _____

What's happening? _____

What's wrong? _____

Who is involved and how? _____

How do you see what's going on? _____

How does the problem affect you? _____

Group brainstorming

Getting a group of involved parties together for brainstorming has some obvious time management advantages. Brainstorming is typically a creative discussion where people build on each other's contributions to produce a comprehensive picture of the situation. As with the interview format, planning is required to make it work. Brainstorming must be led and managed effectively to keep the conversation focused.

The question 'What do we know about this problem?' (or possibly others from the list of questions to uncover problems, page 40) provides the right focal point for group brainstorming as a data collection tool. Do it right and you can help to inspire tremendous creative leaps through joint energy.

Here are some helpful guidelines to apply to your brainstorming sessions. The discussion leader's role takes on added importance if this method is to be successful. If participants edit, judge, react negatively, or just frown at another's contributions, brainstorming breaks down.

Brainstorming guidelines

Question	1.	The discussion leader clearly announces the focus of the session – the key question the group will be answering.
List	2.	The recorder writes down this key question.
Toss out	3.	All participants toss out as many ideas as possible.
Accept	4.	All ideas, however impractical or crazy, are accepted.
Record	5.	The recorder lists all ideas for everyone to see.
Prompt	6.	The discussion leader keeps posing the key question without variation to keep the process on track.
No editing	7.	The discussion leader reminds the participants, as necessary, that no one is allowed to edit, criticise or evaluate any suggestion overtly or covertly until the process is complete.
Build	8.	Participants build on others' ideas. This triggers new thoughts which snowball the group process.

Synergy	9.	By focusing this interaction, the group taps the creative energy of each participant and fuses it in a chain reaction – this is synergy, a combined or cooperative action which is more productive than the sum total of all individual efforts.

Use the brainstorming guidelines and evaluate your success with the following brainstorming checklist.

Brainstorming checklist

Guideline	Yes	No
1. Was the question clearly *presented* and *listed* for all to see?	☐	☐
2. Were participants *drawn out* by noticing their body language and attitudes?	☐	☐
3. Were participants *questioned* and *coaxed* only as needed?	☐	☐
4. Was all *input acknowledged?*	☐	☐
5. Was everyone *encouraged to participate* equally?	☐	☐
6. Did the recorder *write down all new contributions?*	☐	☐
7. Did the group help the recorder to *capture key ideas accurately?*	☐	☐
8. Did the process *stay on track?*	☐	☐
9. Were *ideas constructively built on* by other contributions?	☐	☐
10. Were *new points of view proposed* if the creative flow lagged?	☐	☐
11. Did the discussion leader and recorder *remain neutral* without evaluating or steering the discussion to their own views?	☐	☐
12. Were the ground rules of brainstorming reinforced by immediately *policing any editing, criticism or evaluation?*	☐	☐
13. Did the group *stay stimulated and energised?*	☐	☐
14. Was any *consensus recognised and summed up* when it occured?	☐	☐

CHAPTER 5
Step 2: Problem Labelling

After completing Step 1, you should have a wealth of data on your problem. It may be confusing and you still may not know what kind of problem you have. Group participants may have different interpretations of the same issue.

After a problem recognition session on our Consumer Tech example, some labelled it a manufacturing problem. Others called is a marketing problem. Still others felt it was a petty personality conflict. A management analyst looking from the outside would label it a planning problem. Each reaction has some validity.

A problem will look different from different vantage points. Those doing the looking may label it with different words even though they're talking about the same issue. Whether differences of opinions are about details or major issues, disagreement blocks the necessary teamwork to resolve things.

The Iceberg Rule again
This difference of view can be called the Lifeboat Corollary of the Iceberg Rule. (A corollary is a secondary rule derived from a major principle.)

People in each lifeboat view the obstacle that sank their ocean liner from a different angle. The Lifeboat Corollary says that when this occurs, it is not possible to agree on descriptions. A common example is a manager who says an employee has a negative attitude. Does the employee agree? Not usually. In fact, the result is usually that the worker feels the boss is the one with a distorted outlook.

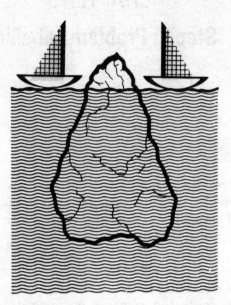

What is a problem label?

Step 2 attempts to identify and label sides of the conflict in a way that everyone can accept. The label can be a phrase that highlights the key issue or the major obstacle. It should describe how things are affected, what needs to change, and the scope of the problem.

For example, everyone in the Consumer Tech situation would agree there was disagreement on how to proceed with the new product feature. One group wanted to introduce the new feature now and the other wanted a more methodical implementation plan.

The result of problem labelling is a simple agreed statement of the common denominators of the problem. You need to identify the central issue that needs resolution: a unifying statement of the main problem.

Why bother?

Why go to the trouble of generating a label? A label functions as a *clear-cut reference point* to focus on during the solution and decision-making process.

The label is like the flag shown below that every lifeboat can see from any direction. The dotted arrow indicates that the function of the label is to lead to the hidden reaches of the iceberg (or problem to be solved).

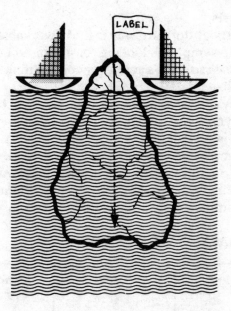

More importantly, all viewpoints must agree on what is to be solved. Outward dissension or internal disagreement at this point will destroy any chance for the logical analysis in Step 3. If those involved can answer 'Yes, that's the problem' to a label, then they *own* their part of the problem. They'll be involved from the inside and really want to help solve the problem.

How to find a problem label

There are four techniques that will help you to find a label for a problem:

1. Data analysis
2. Brainstorming
3. Force-field analysis
4. Key word analysis

Let's take a closer look at each:

Data analysis

The most straightforward way to find a workable label is to sift through the symptoms looking for a common denominator. The *Data analysis work sheet* helps you to think this through. You use it like this:

Fill in key *symptoms* in the left column. Search for patterns. Examine symptoms to identify recurring factors. Categorise symptoms in related groups to identify the *type* of problem at hand. Examples of types are: technical, work habits, interpersonal, organisational, personnel, hardware, political, schedule, financial, service, efficiency, communication etc. Look for common *denominators* until the central issue is clear.

DATA ANALYSIS WORK SHEET

Symptom	Type	Denominators
Common denominators/patterns		

Brainstorming

Use a *Label work sheet* (see page 49) to list possible statements of the problem. One popular question used in brainstorming is: 'How different are things from the way we want them to be?' Other possible target questions are:

What is the problem?
What is the central issue?
How does the present situation differ from the ideal scene?
What do you want to cure or eliminate?
What type of problem are you involved in?
What conflict of ideas of intentions are you involved in?

Be sure you define both sides of the conflict. One way to accomplish this is to define what specific situation you would like to change and what the obstacle is to this change. 'Record-breaking low temperatures during February' isn't a problem until you add 'are killing our birds'. If the second side of the problem was 'are killing elderly citizens who can't afford central heating,' you can see how a label would shift the focus.

The *Sample comments* (page 48) give actual examples of labels developed in problem-solving workshops.

SAMPLE LABEL COMMENTS FROM PROBLEM-SOLVING WORKSHOPS

We can't meet the fixed inflexible customer shipping date for documentation of new software due to continuing engineering changes right up to the last minute.

Lack of communication at shift changeover prevents the next shift from knowing how to handle unresolved problems quickly.

I have a new job and need direction to succeed, but my manager rates me low and doesn't help me improve.

A new software program doesn't meet the specifications and can't be fixed in time to meet the announced one month release date.

I need to work with a colleague, but we can't stand one another.

An accounting program is needed for regular invoices produced on time, but no matter what's done to fix it, the program keeps going down.

I keep getting more work assignments than can be handled properly and at once, but all of them are assigned 'number one priority' with a due date of 'as soon as possible'.

We need to sort out a customer's problem on the phone but he or she is too emotional to give the facts.

Label work sheet

Force-field analysis

A two-column force-field analysis process helps to identify a label for a problem. Two suggested applications are presented, an *A versus B* format and an *Obstacles* format.

The *A versus B* format generates a label which defines two conflicting forces. For example:

'We should introduce the new product feature right away *versus* we should proceed carefully until we handle manufacturing and stock problems.'

The *Obstacles* format lets you list what you want or what you need and then what prevents you from getting it. For example:

'We want to introduce the new product feature right away, but quality problems *prevent* this from being a good idea.'

FORCE-FIELD ANALYSIS
'A versus B'

What do you want?	What don't you want?

FORCE-FIELD ANALYSIS
'Obstacles'

How do you want things to be? What do you need?	What obstacles prevent you from getting it?

Key word analysis

Key word analysis is a method of defining pivotal or disputed words or concepts. Communication is critical to effect problem-solving and decision-making and semantics sometimes become a barrier. Semantic problems occur when different people have different meanings for the same words. Using the *Key word analysis work sheet* on page 53 will clarify disputed words and terms to help clearer and more acceptable labels to be devised.

To conduct a key word analysis:

- Select the word/term that seems to cause the problem.
- Write it in the top box of the worksheet.
- Have the group define this key word specifically in as many ways as possible.
- Select one meaning everyone agrees on and include that definition in your label, or replace the offending word in your original label with a more acceptable word.

In the Consumer Tech case, *quality* is an interesting word to define. Here are the initial reactions from members of the staff.

SAMPLE KEY WORD ANALYSIS WORK SHEET

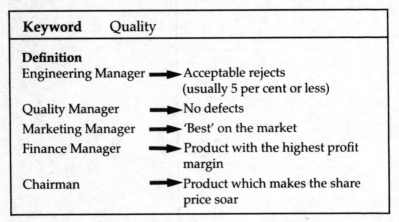

Keyword	Quality
Definition	
Engineering Manager ➡	Acceptable rejects (usually 5 per cent or less)
Quality Manager ➡	No defects
Marketing Manager ➡	'Best' on the market
Finance Manager ➡	Product with the highest profit margin
Chairman ➡	Product which makes the share price soar

Key word analysis is only a supporting technique that provides problem-solvers and decision-makers with a valuable troubleshooting tool.

KEY WORD ANALYSIS WORK SHEET

Key word

Define the key word as specifically as possible in as many ways as you can

Test your work

Regardless of which method you use to arrive at a label, it's a good idea to test its effectiveness before proceeding. The problem label test summarises what makes an effective label. Run down the list, evaluate your proposed label, and adjust it accordingly. Experience has shown that inadequate labelling is one of the biggest reasons for poor problem definition.

Problem label test

Does the label . . .	Yes	No
Define what you want to solve?	☐	☐
State generally what aspect of the problem you want to cure?	☐	☐
Explain precisely what you want to change?	☐	☐
Identify both sides of the conflict?	☐	☐
Define what the obstacle is to what goal?	☐	☐
State the central, key issue?	☐	☐
Clearly and specifically document the dilemma?	☐	☐
Define the type of problem you're dealing with?	☐	☐
Generate agreement from all sides of the conflict?	☐	☐
Identify the ownership of the problem (who *has* it)?	☐	☐

CHAPTER 6

Step 3: The Problem Cause Analysis

Problem cause analysis produces the true problem definition. So why have we taken valuable time with Steps 1 and 2? Because it is extremely difficult to sort through the mental and emotional issues that cloud a problem. Previous steps helped to create general awareness of what the problem is and isn't. These steps helped to sort out the *causes* (contributing forces or stimuli that raised the problem in the first place) from the *effects*, the symptoms, and by-products of the causes.

Step 3 looks for the *root cause* of the problem. The root cause is a controllable, soluble force which explains why the problem exists. Chester Barnard, an early author on the process of management, called this 'the limiting factor'. As chief executive of a large regional telephone company several decades ago, he found that the only problems which reached his desk were ones with a missing link. When he was able to ferret out this missing link or limiting factor, a problem could finally be resolved once and for all.

That iceberg again
A dentist once pointed out that the term *root cause* doesn't fit the image of the Iceberg Rule. Well, perhaps, but the picture still demonstrates that we're searching for the basic core of the iceberg.

During Step 3 you will identify contributing forces that make the problem worse, sort through partial explanations that are possible causes, and weed out the by-product effects. You might think you've found the answer too soon. As you

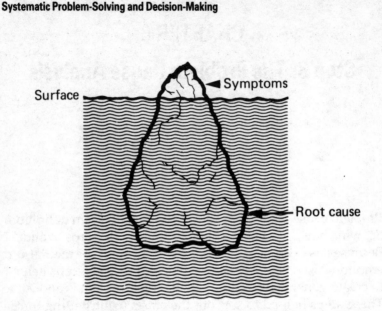

analyse your answers, the layers beneath the surface show that partial explanations are often found for why the problem exists. The root cause is at the bottom. It's the pivotal reason that started the problem in the first place and must be dealt with in order to find a long-term workable solution.

A specific example

The layers beneath the surface of the iceberg illustrate a significant feature of the anatomy of problems. Typically, people try to fix the superficial symptoms or partial explanations which stem from the root cause. For example:

A worker hears a rumour from an inside source about plant closings and assumes the worst – 'I'm going to lose my job.' Even though it isn't true, it creates insecurity, so the worker puts out feelers for a new job. A supervisor hears about it and starts giving the cold shoulder to the seemingly disloyal employee. If job offers fall through, the worker is now stuck with bad working conditions.

The employee may not understand this compounding sequence or be able to communicate with the supervisor about the foolish assumption that was made. Or the worker may feel the need to protect an inside source.

The layers look like this, with the latest symptoms on top and the more fundamental causes below:

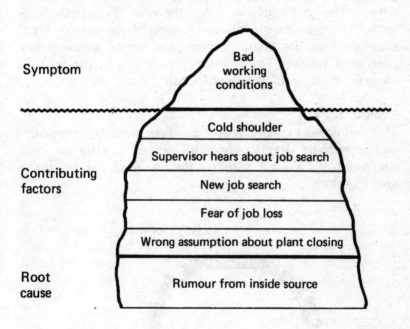

Symptom	Bad working conditions
	Cold shoulder
	Supervisor hears about job search
Contributing factors	New job search
	Fear of job loss
	Wrong assumption about plant closing
Root cause	Rumour from inside source

If this snowballing series of events was openly examined it could be cleared up. A little temporary embarrassment might remain but no permanent damage would be done.

You can handle it
Sometimes problem cause analysis yields a root cause that seems insoluble. This factor can't be the actual root cause because it's not a controllable force that can be dealt with.

Some years ago an insurance branch office ran into severe cash problems early in the spring. The causes were traced back to a snowstorm at the company headquarters some weeks earlier. During the extreme winter weather, no one could get to work and the post was held up for several days.

Was the weather the root cause? Absolutely not. It was a partial explanation, but why should a freeze-up, not uncommon at that time of year, suddenly cripple the branch? The problem cause analysis showed that cash wasn't managed properly to prepare for this worst case scenario that winter. The root cause was that the branch controller was without a replacement while recuperating from surgery. Until someone took the financial reins (and maybe a new policy prevented unfilled key employee positions in the future), more financial problems would result.

Remove the key
The root cause explains why a problem persists, reappears, and repeatedly draws people into stress, frustration, and confusion. It's like a keystone – the one brick that holds the arch together.

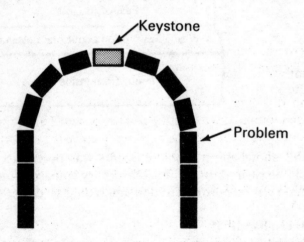

Find the keystone, remove it with a good solution, and the problem will collapse.

When those involved have an uplifting 'Aha!' experience that fully explains the situation, you've found the root cause.

'Aha' is a term for the moment of recognition and realisation. Often the keystone of a problem is right under your nose, but you didn't notice how important that particular factor was.

The Consumer Tech root cause

When Consumer Tech's management team analysed their disagreement on how to proceed with the new product, they found many contributing factors. Ultimately it was traced to the board of directors and some over-optimistic preliminary reports about the successful test results of the new toothbrush. The board was wildly excited about the potential effect on the share price if the product hit the market ahead of the competition.

This explained the source of the underlying pressure to introduce the new toothbrush immediately. But the board didn't have the whole story. Several quality and stock issues remained unresolved. So the root cause was defined as:

> An incomplete briefing of the board regarding the Electronic Toothbrush.

How did this happen? Some enthusiastic staff members passed initial glowing reports to the board. This is no crime in an open shop. It is natural to want to spread good news to higher-ups. No one is to blame for the root cause. That's not the point. The purpose of problem cause analysis is to learn what happened so that successful corrective action can be taken.

Note how different this root cause is from unilateral pressures to resolve the problem. These forces contributed to why the problem existed and partially explained why it persisted. But they weren't enough. That's the power of the root cause. You find a missing explanation that everyone can acknowledge and you finally have a chance of a lasting solution.

Unfortunately, just handling the root cause – giving the board the whole story now – won't solve the entire problem. But until they have been briefed completely, no problem resolution is likely.

Distinguishing cause from effect

During Step 3 you analyse the data you have collected or need to research. Then you look for cause/effect relationships until you find the most fundamental underlying cause. You keep turning over stones and looking underneath until there's nothing left to discover.

Sometimes distinguishing cause from effect is tricky. The dictionary defines a cause as 'anything which produces an effect' and an effect as 'something which is produced by a cause'. Big help, right? It helps to think of *causes* as forces that create or worsen problem symptoms, and *effects* as the consequences resulting from causes. But when you're lost between the top and bottom of an iceberg, cause and effect can be confusing.

Try out the cause/effect analysis exercise on page 61 to assess and sharpen your skills. This situation analyses the dilemma of a computer programmer in the Engineering Department of Consumer Tech who is leading the development of a new application. The lead programmer refused to accept the results of the code review. This is a meeting in which a program is gone over with a fine tooth comb to see if it will do what's intended. Can you tell cause from effect?

Cause/effect analysis exercise

Label. Lead programmer disagrees with results of recent code review.

Directions. Classify the following factors as either cause (C) or effect (E). Check the answers at the bottom of the page to see if you labelled the factors correctly.

Factor	Cause (C) or effect (E)
1. Heated words recently between programmers.	_____
2. Different programming methods used prior to review.	_____
3. Programmer frustrated since new programming methods introduced.	_____
4. No training in new methods.	_____
5. Lack of supervision by lead programmer.	_____
6. Name calling during code review.	_____
7. Lead programmer given 'do it your own way' authority.	_____
8. Old database design selected.	_____
9. 280 hours to fix bugs found in code review.	_____
10. No one enjoys working with lead programmer.	_____
11. Extra staff added as result of poor progress.	_____
12. Lead programmer displayed a 'know it all' attitude.	_____
13. Little user input considered in design of new code.	_____

Answers. The following factors were causes: 2, 4, 5, 7, 8, 12 and 13. The remaining factors were effects.

How to find the root cause

By this point in our PS/DM outline, you have identified quite a few causes. If you've documented Steps 1 and 2 for your Personal Case Problem, you need to review the facts, symptoms, proposed labels, and key word definitions, searching for contributing forces. Transfer the causes you've already identified to the *Cause analysis work sheet*. This can be a major time saver, but requires the ability to tell causes from effects. If you can't distinguish between cause and effect you'll end up transferring too many items.

CAUSE ANALYSIS WORK SHEET

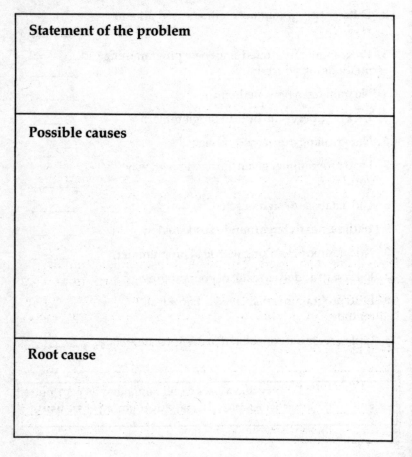

Statement of the problem

Possible causes

Root cause

Six techniques to identify problem causes

Problem cause analysis is probably the most demanding action of the entire PS/DM outline.

The six techniques listed below can help. Each will be reviewed individually.

1. Brainstorming
2. Positive/negative forces analysis
3. Charting unknowns
4. Chronological analysis
5. Repetitive why analysis
6. Cause/effect diagram

1. Brainstorming

You can add to your list of potential root causes by brainstorming. Possible questions to use as your focal point are:

What caused the problem?
Why does the problem exist?
Where did it start and where did it come from?
Why doesn't it resolve itself or just go away?
What caused it in the first place?
What changed just before things went wrong?
Why do you keep getting sucked back into the situation?
Why don't things improve, no matter what is done?

2. Positive/negative forces analysis

The now familiar two column work sheet, *Positive/negative forces analysis for causes*, can be used to stimulate thinking to add to the list of causes. By going back and forth from what minimises the trouble to what makes it worse, new contributing forces are identified that didn't occur to anyone before.

POSITIVE/NEGATIVE FORCES ANALYSIS FOR CAUSES

What forces lessen or minimise the problem?	What forces worsen or contribute to the problem?
(Use the above headings to	create your own work sheet.)

3. Charting unknowns

Sometimes problem-solving and decision-making groups run dry before they really look comprehensively at the issue. To break through these blind spots, use the *Charting unknowns work sheet* to energise creative thinking. In a sense, this is just another brainstorming question but applied with reverse psychology. Mental blocks may develop from concentrating too hard on what you do know about the problem. By asking, 'What don't we know about the problem?' you may cause hidden facts to emerge or new research directions to be suggested.

CHARTING UNKNOWNS WORK SHEET

Statement of the problem
What is not known about the problem?

4. Chronological analysis

The layered drawing of the iceberg shows how unsolved problems evolve. A bad decision causes a production problem. A first-aid solution works temporarily, but creates side-effects. Quick fixes are found for these by-products but they are temporary. Months later no one remembers where it all started.

Using the chronological problem analysis, it is possible to recall the sequence of events leading up to the situation. Starting from present time, list the major symptoms or causes and examine when each started. This type of investigation reveals cause/effect relationships by identifying what happened before the last crisis. Often you find that an intermediate problem was actually caused by an inappropriate solution made earlier.

CHRONOLOGICAL PROBLEM ANALYSIS WORK SHEET

Major symptom/cause	When did it start?	What happened then?
(Use the above headings to create your own work sheet.)		

On the *Chronological problem analysis work sheet*, the causes from the Consumer Tech programmer's disagreement were listed in chronological order with the most recent cause at the top.

Lack of supervision of programming team.
Lead programmer selected old database design.
Different programming methods used prior to review.
Little user input considered in design of new code.
No training on new methods.
Lead programmer given 'do it your own way' authority.
Lead programmer displayed a 'know it all' attitude.

In this particular case it was apparent that the lead programmer's attitude was a personality trait that wasn't about to change. The final analysis showed that giving a 'know it all' do it your own way authority was what really precipitated the continuing troubles. This is not to point the finger of blame. Some decisions look like the most expedient solution at the time but later breed other trouble. Hindsight is the best teacher, so put your emphasis on *what*, not *who*.

It helps to plot the results of this analysis on a *Problem timeline*. This sample gives you an idea of what such a chart looks like. The clear picture may not answer any specific questions itself, but it shows what to ignore and exactly where to look when you're searching for the root cause.

LEAD PROGRAMMER PROBLEM TIMELINE

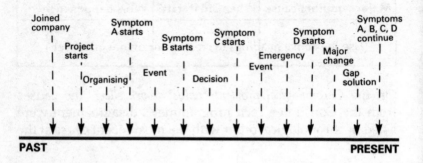

5. Repetitive why analysis

Extensive analysis sometimes generates many potential causes but no clear 'Aha!' regarding the root. It helps to trace the evolution of the problem with a *Repetitive why analysis*. This procedure distinguishes between the most fundamental causes and their intermediate effects. The logic process used strongly resembles the idea of uncovering a piece of paper which hides another piece of paper, hiding another etc.

If the root cause doesn't appear during your initial search, find one underlying factor that seems to be most fundamental. Write it in the first box of the *Repetitive why work sheet*. Then ask, 'What caused that?' or 'Why is that a problem?' repeatedly until you locate the basic factor on the chain. An example follows to show how this works.

REPETITIVE WHY WORK SHEET

Problem:

```
┌──────────────────────────────────────────┐
│                                            │
│                                            │
│                                            │
└──────────────────────────────────────────┘
```

Which was caused by . . .

```
┌──────────────────────────────────────────┐
│                                            │
│                                            │
│                                            │
└──────────────────────────────────────────┘
```

66

Which was caused by . . .

Which was caused by . . .

Which was caused by . . .

REPETITIVE WHY WORK SHEET – SAMPLE

Problem: *Irate customer on the phone*

Fifth time put on hold.

Which was caused by . . .

Inability to get new telephone system to work as designed.

Which was caused by . . .

Incorrect written instructions about process.

Which was caused by . . .

Wrong instruction manual in box with new phone.

Which was caused by . . .

Temporary packers taken on to cover holiday period didn't have written policy to follow and inserted wrong manual in product package.

6. Cause/effect diagram

Another way to think through a problem cause analysis logically is to create a Cause/effect diagram. This is often called a fishbone diagram because its lines resemble that of a discarded skeleton after a good fish dinner. The diagram visually categorises forces into related groups for simpler analysis.

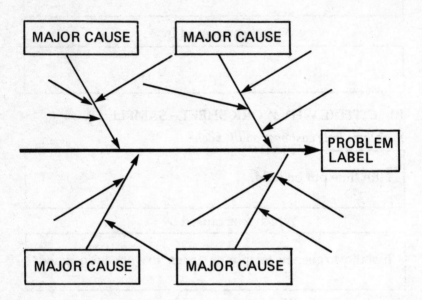

Here is what a cause/effect diagram for Consumer Tech would look like:

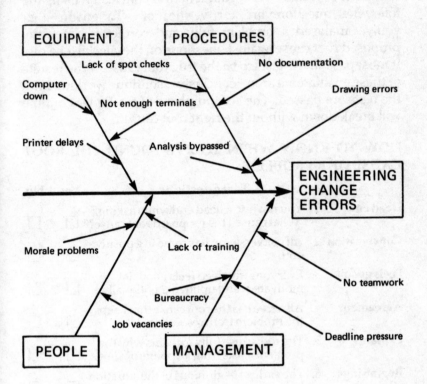

Have you found the root cause?

Don't move to the solution phase until you are sure you have found the root cause. Test your tentative conclusion using the following questionnaire for verification. To ensure that you've analysed a problem fully and correctly, check the proposed root cause against questions on the checklist below. It must pass *all* the tests to be the true root cause. If the results of these evaluations aren't conclusive, continue working until the tests are passed. The second phase of the PS/DM outline will break down without the right root cause.

HOW TO KNOW WHEN YOU'VE FOUND THE ROOT CAUSE OF A PROBLEM

	Test questions	Yes	No
Dead end	1. You ran into a dead end when asking, 'What caused the proposed root cause?'	☐	☐
Conversation	2. All conversation has come to a positive end.	☐	☐
Feels good	3. Everyone involved feels good, is motivated, and uplifted emotionally.	☐	☐
Agreement	4. All agree it is the root cause that keeps the problem from resolution.	☐	☐
Explains	5. The root cause fully explains why the problem exists from all points of view.	☐	☐
Beginnings	6. The earliest beginnings of the situation have been explored and understood.	☐	☐
Logical	7. The root cause is logical, make sense, and dispels all confusion.	☐	☐
Control	8. The root cause is something you can influence, control and deal with realistically.	☐	☐
Hope	9. Finding the root cause has returned hope that something constructive can be done about the situation.	☐	☐
Workable solution	10. Suddenly workable solutions, not outrageous demands, that deal with all the symptoms begin to appear.	☐	☐
Stable resolution	11. A stable, long-term, once and for all resolution of the situation now appears feasible.	☐	☐

When should you do what?
Step 3 is the most demanding and confusing step in the PS/DM process. More options are presented here than anywhere else in the PS/DM outline. This wealth of tools sometimes overwhelms problem-solvers and decision-makers. The *Root cause analysis programme* is a general sequence of techniques which serves as a starting point agenda.

Adjust the order of steps to best approach your situation.

ROOT CAUSE ANALYSIS PROGRAMME CHECKLIST

		Date completed
Process	1. Agree on which process the group is using at each point in the analysis.	_____
Roles	2. Select an appropriate discussion leader and recorder.	_____
Brainstorm	3. First brainstorm an appropriate question, then document all answers on a simple form such as the *Cause analysis work sheet* on page 62.	_____
+/− Forces	4. Use a *Positive/negative forces analysis* to add to your list of possible causes.	_____
Evaluate	5. Evaluate which cause is most fundamental and underlying all others.	_____
Diagram	6. Group or categorise the possible causes and determine which category is most basic, using a *Cause/effect diagram*.	_____
Repetitive why	7. Use the *Repetitive why work sheet* to trace the most basic cause down to its root. If you hit a dead end, try another starting point down a different path.	_____
Others	8. Use other techniques to add to or evaluate the possible causes on your list until you identify the root cause.	_____

		Date completed

Test   9. When you think you've got it, test your hypothesis using the checklist *How to know when you've found the root cause of a problem* (page 70).   _____

Persevere   10. If your first hypothesis doesn't work out, go back and continue your analysis until you succeed. It will be a frustrating waste of time if you skip to solving the problem without an 'Aha!' experience at this point.   _____

CHAPTER 7
Step 4: Optional Solutions

Finally, work can begin on the second phase of the PS/DM outline, problem-solving. Deciding on a workable solution for the root cause begins with Step 4. This is not a lengthy or complicated step, but is vital in generating agreement on the ultimate decision.

Step 4 is called *optional solutions* because the goal is to complete a list of conceivable alternatives. You're looking for any strategies which will address the root cause and resolve the problem once and for all. A complete list of alternatives is essential before proceeding to Step 5.

Why as long a list as possible?
Insisting on a comprehensive list prevents you from rushing off impulsively with the first idea that sounds good. There's a chance that if you follow the first off-the-cuff proposal, it will be inferior, inadequate, or unbalanced. You've come this far by avoiding short-cuts. Don't give in to the temptation now.

Draw on the creative powers of those involved to examine all possible courses of action. This will ensure that all views are considered. Although this may not be enough to preclude differences of opinion during decision-making, it at least creates the respect and acceptance so often missing in conflict situations. Everyone may have his or her own hidden agenda and/or pet solution, so be sure to get these in the open and on the list.

Once you get agreement that every course of action is on the list and will be considered, a group will feel some direct ownership in the decision-making process. And this may help to put the group in the mood to generate consensus later.

The Consumer Tech case problem unfolds

Consumer Tech came up with the following list of options (in no particular sequence) to solve the problem of their Electronic Toothbrush:

1. Let the Chairman make the decision and then get the dissenters in line.
2. Replace those who want to introduce the new toothbrush immediately.
3. Start a spin-off operation to produce a model with the new feature.
4. Replace those who want to go more slowly.
5. Threaten to resign as a protest about pressure from the board of directors.
6. Schedule a meeting with the board to make sure they have the necessary information and let them make the final decision.
7. Develop a joint planning process involving the board.
8. Let the current thrashing process work itself out (do nothing).
9. Hire a consultant to mediate the process.

Some of the above are more sensible than others. The 'replacement' options (2 and 4) are downright threatening, but the Consumer Tech management team included them to make the list complete. Once the list is complete, there should be one thing less to argue about, namely: 'Is the best solution on the list?' If they have done their job, the solution will be on the list.

Building a complete list

The following three techniques will generate a complete list of optional solutions:

1. Recovery
2. Brainstorming
3. Force-field analysis

These techniques are designed to identify strategic directions and basic approaches, not specific tasks. To list every helpful action would make the task monumental. Apply a 'seeing the wood, not the trees' concept. If you come up with a large number of action tasks instead of strategies, save them for action planning at Step 6.

1. Recovery

The obvious starting place is to review your notes. The temptation to get rid of symptoms during problem analysis is great. You will probably have many possible solutions in your notes from Steps 1, 2, and 3. If so, you have a head start on Step 4. Here is an example of how careful documentation and thorough analysis pays off.

Recover any potential solution strategies discovered earlier and transfer them to the *Optional solutions work sheet* on page 76. These may have been ideas on how to resolve the situation, or they may represent actual past attempts to deal with the problem. Since the motto is 'Anything goes', previous attempts need to be on the list. An earlier flop may work if better focused, or old ideas may suggest more workable variations.

OPTIONAL SOLUTIONS WORK SHEET

Root cause to solve	
List all strategies that have any chance of working	**Evaluation (Step 5)***

* Leave the evaluation column blank until Step 5.

2: Brainstorming

Brainstorming seems to have been made for Step 4. Concentrate on conceiving any strategies that have the slightest chance of resolving the root cause. Consider incredible proposals, ridiculous or unacceptable approaches, all 'far-out' suggestions, and anything pertaining to the resolution of the underlying issue.

Research on meetings shows that conservative groups are much less effective in problem resolution than those willing to consider wild-eyed schemes. Removing blinkers and internal barriers may generate some crazy ideas. Typically, even harebrained proposals can often be moulded into workable methods no one would have dreamed of without unrestrained brainstorming.

Add to your *Optional solutions work sheet* as things progress. Be sure to follow the rules of brainstorming and avoid editing or evaluating until the list is complete. Always include *doing nothing* as one option since this course of action should be consciously considered.

Possible target questions to serve as the focal point for this process are:

What would solve the problem?
What strategy could resolve the root cause?
What solutions have already been thought of?
What approaches haven't been thought of?
How could we stop this situation from recurring?
What different methods might work?
What crazy ideas might help?

3. Force-field analysis

The *Positive/Negative analysis for solutions* can stimulate thinking just as the force-field format did in the past. Since we're looking for solutions, the two columns play *better* against *worse*. This is similar to the work sheet in Step 3 designed to generate causes. New approaches should be added to the master list of optional solutions.

POSITIVE/NEGATIVE FORCES ANALYSIS FOR SOLUTIONS

What would make the problem better?	What would make the problem worse?

CHAPTER 8
Step 5: Decision-Making

Decision-making is the second half of the title of this book. Yet it's taken us a long time to get here. That's because everything up to this point is designed to make decision-making work properly.

Step 5 allows you to choose one alternative solution as a course of action. You make a value judgement on what to do about the problem. The result you want is a firm joint decision on the chosen optional solution. This means selecting one strategy from the list in Step 4 that everyone will respect.

Too often decision-making consists of abuse of political power, personal preference, poor leadership, or a macho demonstration of decisiveness. The PS/DM process is designed to avoid these. Having analysed the problem thoroughly, determined the underlying root cause, and listed possible alternatives allows the problem-solver/decision-maker to make an objective, rational, comparative evaluation.

Evaluate choices

The philosophy of Step 5 is *evaluation*. This means lining up your ducks, eliminating the worst choices and weighing remaining choices against each other. You will consider ranking, prioritising, and scoring the alternatives to make your choices. The goal is to find the 'right' solution using a practical, scientific process.

There are several approaches to solving a problem. The team-building/conflict-resolution process built into the PS/DM outline is recommended. Those involved 'own' a portion of the analysis since they participated in its conclusions. Every realistic strategy should be on the list of options. People will continue to have preferences and different points of view. What helps the organisation in the long run may hurt an individual or department in the short run. Trade-offs may have to be made. Differing viewpoints always suggest compromise. People may bargain, exchange favours, or apply pressure.

You've worked hard to set things up for an objective comparison, and you're in a good position to pull it off. Remember that the primary concern is to make a firm choice that everybody buys. If they support it, it will work and the implementation that you'll design in Step 6 will be carried out.

A 'right' decision may exist; however, it will not work unless those involved 'buy in'. A compromise choice may be less risky, and more popular. A secondary workable solution that is agreed is better than a 'perfect choice' that continues to create controversy from hidden resistance. So a pragmatic subjective choice is required as well as a 'right' objective one. *Once your decision is chosen and agreed to, it is essential to keep to it.*

How to make a decision

Following are eight decision-making tools. These are presented in order from the least structured to the most structured:

1. Informal discussion
2. Brainstorming
3. Elimination
4. Weighing against goals
5. Weighing against consequences
6. Prioritising
7. Combination
8. Criteria matrix

1. Informal discussion

It is natural to discuss a list of options first. Thinking out loud, bouncing ideas off an interested sounding board, and getting advantages and disadvantages in the open is a healthy starting point for a decision. You can record any conclusions in the evaluation column of the *Optional solutions work sheet* from Step 4. This tool is the least structured process for evaluating options, but it plays a critical role in problem-solving and decision-making.

2. Brainstorming

Brainstorming wasn't designed for objective decision-making. The momentum of group thinking can sway rational analysis away from a balanced evaluation. But it can be an effective method. Possible questions to use as guidelines are:

How does each alternative solution measure up?
Which option seems most workable?
Which solution has the best chance of success?
How risky is each possible solution?
Which solution can everyone decide to fully commit to?
Which solution do you definitely choose?

3. Elimination

It is common during informal discussion or brainstorming to discover that some options won't work. Eliminating unworkable choices can reduce a long list to something more manageable. You can delete items using specific disqualifying factors such as, cost, risk or time. The following tools may be difficult with an unwieldy list.

Put an 'X' next to the options you would eliminate from the list Consumer Tech generated. Then check the answers with those in the upside down box below to see which options Consumer Tech eliminated.

1. Let the Chairman decide and then get the dissenters in line _____

2. Replace those who want to introduce the new toothbrush now _____

3. Start a spin-off operation to produce a model with the new feature _____

4. Replace those who want to go more slowly _____

5. Threaten to resign in protest at board pressure _____

6. Fully brief the board and let them decide _____

7. Develop a joint planning process involving the board _____

8. Let the current thrashing process work itself out (do nothing) _____

9. Hire a consultant to mediate the process. _____

> **ANSWERS.** During the decision-making process, Consumer Tech quickly ruled 2, 4 and 5 as clearly undesirable.

4. Weighing against goals

Review your list of remaining options and weigh them against the goals of the organisation, department, or personal performance plan. For this to be successful, an accurate, up-to-date strategic plan is required. Problem-solving and decision-making groups often find it necessary to develop or refine organisational or personal goals at this point.

A useful approach to tool 4 is first to develop a statement of an ideal situation: how you would want things to be if you had total control over circumstances. Then evaluate your alternative solutions against this scenario.

5. Weighing against consequences

You can weigh the potential ramifications of each option using the *Consequences work sheet* below. List key solutions in the left column and then predict the likely consequences in the columns to the right. By comparing the contents of one column against the next, you create a risk/reward and cost/benefit analysis. In the conclusions column, decide whether

the possible benefits and rewards justify the potential costs
and risks.

CONSEQUENCES WORK SHEET

Solution	Potential costs	Potential risks	Possible benefits	Possible rewards	Conclusions

6. Prioritising

The *Prioritising methods checklist* offers six approaches to selecting the best solution from a list. Each method has its strengths. Decide which method you think will work best and apply it to your list of options.

A second method you may not be familiar with is bubble up/bubble down. It functions like a computer sorting device. In a forced-pair comparison, you take the first two items on the list and decide which is better. If the second wins, it moves to the top of the list. Otherwise leave them as is and move to the next distinct pair. As an example let's use the remaining items in the Consumer Tech list.

1. Let the Chairman decide and get the dissenters in line
3. Start a spin-off operation to produce a model with the new feature
6. Fully brief the board and let them decide
7. Develop a joint planning process involving the board
8. Let the current thrashing process work itself out (do nothing)
9. Hire a consultant to mediate the process

(1 and 3 seem to be in the right order, so leave them as is.)

When we compare 3 and 6, the spin-off option seems less desirable and should move down.

1. Let the Chairman decide and get the dissenters in line
6. Fully brief the board and let them decide
3. Start a spin-off operation to produce a model with the new feature
7. Develop a joint planning process involving the board
8. Let the current thrashing process work itself out (do nothing)
9. Hire a consultant to mediate the process

This process should continue for all items on the list. A forced-pair prioritising comparison is finished when there is agreement on the relative position of every item on the list in relation to every other item.

Do you agree with the final order below from the Consumer Tech case or would you organise them differently?

7. Develop a joint planning process involving the board
6. Fully brief the board and let them decide
9. Hire a consultant to mediate the process
1. Let the Chairman decide and get the dissenters in line
3. Start a spin-off operation to produce a model with the new feature
8. Let the current thrashing process work itself out (do nothing)

PRIORITISING METHODS CHECKLIST

1. Ranking in order of: _____
     Best   _____
     Most workable   _____
     Reliability   _____
     Most tested and proven   _____
     Least risky   _____
     Staff ability to make it work   _____
     Chance of success   _____

2. Use forced-pair comparison to
   bubble up/bubble down items
   resulting in a prioritised list.   _____

3. Get individuals in a group to rate
   each item and then tabulate ratings
   using a scale such as: _____
       5 = Top preference
       4 = High preference
       3 = OK
       2 = Maybe
       1 = Slim chance
       0 = No chance

4. Vote where majority rules.   _____

5. Prioritise by gut feel, intuition, or comfort zone. _____

6. Compromise.   _____

7. Combination

At some point during evaluation, problem-solvers and decision-makers may find that two or more items on the list do not conflict. Solutions that complement each other could work well together. A useful decision-making technique is to categorise remaining options. By combining solutions within a category, it is possible to shorten the list for your final choice. Pool creative thinking on each alternative within a category for more workable outcomes. Decision-making then boils down to a more simple job of comparing categories.

The top three options on the Consumer Tech list aren't mutually exclusive. In fact, all have benefits. After some consideration, the management team decided to combine items 7, 6 and 9. Their list now reads like this:

7/6/9. Hire a consultant mediator, fully brief the board and develop a joint planning process with the board.

1. Let the Chairman decide and get the dissenters in line.
3. Start a spin-off operation to produce a model with the new feature.
8. Let the current thrashing process work itself out (do nothing).

---

8. Criteria matrix

A helpful method to visualise decision choices is a criteria matrix. This is a chart with alternative solutions listed in the left column and the criteria to measure them across the top.

To use the criteria matrix, you must first develop a thoughtful *Standards and criteria list*. Criteria are accepted standards, common-sense benchmarks or proved yardsticks that indicate what an effective solution would look like. Make a list of measurement indicators that tell whether a proposed solution is good, bad, or marginal.

You may wish to consider what organisational goals, departmental objectives and job targets are affected by the problem. Do validated quality or quantity standards exist? Take into account any time, cost, material, or human constraints or limitations that need to be considered. What negative consequences should your choice avoid at all costs? Look for benchmarks against which to judge the workability of the items on your list of alternative solutions.

Consumer Tech's management group developed the following list of criteria:

STANDARDS AND CRITERIA LIST

By what standards and criteria should you judge your optional strategies?

Effect on share price

Expansion of market

Cost-effectiveness

Effect on management and staff morale

Level of risk

The alternative solutions are listed in the left-hand column of the matrix, with the criteria listed across the top. It is important to use a key word or phrase. If you use lengthy statements or numbers, the matrix won't communicate visually what you are evaluating.

You can rate options using a +, −, ?, scale, an **A,B,C** label, or a numeric scale of **1 to 3** or **1 to 10**. When using the numeric scale, add up each row to generate a numeric score for each alternative. A weighted evaluation can also be used to give a different multiplier to scores under each criteria. With or without weighting, the final ranking comes from adding the ratings in each row. The matrix is helpful in compartmentalising a complex analysis. But the answer is no more accurate than the individual scores. Other methods of rating may be more appropriate in specific cases. Be sure to define your scale in the box at the top of the matrix before you begin.

CRITERIA MATRIX

Rating scale:

Alternative solutions		Evaluation criteria					R A T I N G

In the resulting boxes, you rate each option against each criterion. We'll see how Consumer Tech rated their alternative solutions on page 89.

Consumer Tech chose a 5-point scale. Based on your knowledge of the case, rate the options and add up the scores as you see it. Then compare your ratings with those of Consumer Tech which appear on page 90.

CONSUMER TECH CRITERIA MATRIX

Rating scale: 1 to 5, with 5 = best

Alternative Solutions		SHARE	MARKET	COST	MORALE	RISK		RATING
		Evaluation criteria						
7/6/9. Consultant mediator/board briefing/joint planning process								
1. Chairman decides and gets dissenters in line								
3. Start a spin-off operation to produce a model with the new feature								
8. Let the current thrashing process work itself out (do nothing)								

THE CONSUMER TECH RANKING

Here's how Consumer Tech scored their remaining options:

Alternative Solutions	Evaluation criteria					
	S H A R E	M A R K E T	C O S T	M O R A L E	R I S K	R A T I N G
7/6/9. Consultant mediator/board briefing/joint planning process	5	5	4	5	5	24
1. Chairman decides and gets dissenters in line	2	3	5	3	3	16
3. Start a spin-off operation to produce a model with the new feature	4	5	1	4	1	15
8. Let the current thrashing process work itself out (do nothing)	1	3	5	1	1	11

In this case, the bubble-up/bubble-down process yielded the same result as a criteria matrix. This is a good double check. In real life you probably wouldn't apply every decision-making tool. Some will be more appropriate than others. Use your judgement.

The final score for each alternative is only as reliable as the accuracy of each individual rating. This process only breaks down a complex evaluation into a series of smaller judgements. So if the top scores are close, don't make your final decision solely on the results of matrix.

Decision Test

Evaluate your final choice with a decision test. This is done by designing questions to test the workability of your key solutions. When evaluating a decision, the form below will determine whether you've picked the ideal decision, the decision most likely to succeed, or the most workable decision. The ideal decision will pass all tests, but may not be workable. In decision-making, perfection is secondary to workability.

DECISION TEST

Test question	Yes	No?
1. Does it solve the problem and the root cause?		
2. Does it satisfy all established criteria?		
3. Does it satisfy all people involved and affected?		
4. Can workable action plans be developed to implement it?		
5. Is there time to implement it?		
6. Do the personnel and resources exist to make it work?		
7. Will its implementation end recurrence of the problem?		
8. Have all its risks, disadvantages, and possible consequences been considered?		
9. Is it the best choice in terms of:		
(a) Benefits		
(b) Costs		
(c) Risks		
(d) Commitment		
(e) Workability?		

CHAPTER 9
Step 6: Action Planning

The best solution ever conceived and agreed won't solve a problem if it isn't put into action. An action plan details who will do what, by when. An action plan organises tasks which implement the decision in the real world. Timing, personnel and other resources must be considered and choreographed into action. Setting performance standards, production and quality targets, plus a follow-up monitoring mechanism, is vital to ensure that the plan is carried through.

Murphy's Law
Always consider Murphy's Law: That which can go wrong, will. No matter how well you predict the future, think through the sequence of implementation, or estimate time and resources; your plan will rarely go as conceived. It is better to anticipate problems and prepare as best you can. The best action plans include contingency thinking to avoid Murphy's worst effects.

Is it worth the trouble?
New managers often ask, 'Why bother to plan at all?' The answer is simple: with a plan you will be much better prepared to adapt and respond even when things go wrong. Action planning allows for fast adjustment and wise reaction, not a rigid inflexible pattern for the future.

The value of action planning

Benefits are included in the checklist below. Tick off those items which would help you to implement decisions and solutions.

Value of action planning checklist		Agree
Realistic actions	1. They translate decisions into workable realistic actions staff can identify with.	
Concrete programmes	2. They nail down abstract ideas into concrete programmes which are achievable.	
Specific assignments	3. They give specific assignments so that individuals know what to do and when.	
Clear expectations	4. They create clear expectations so staff know how they will be evaluated.	
Effective delegation	5. They divide responsibility for effective delegation in a simple way.	
Mutual commitment	6. They build agreement by establishing mutual commitment to the plan.	
Coordinate action	7. They coordinate action and thus contribute to team-building and team-work.	
Effective follow-up	8. They provide an effective follow-up mechanism by mapping future check-points.	
Objective measurement	9. They establish a basis for objective results measurement.	
Clear-cut accountability	10. They contribute to clear-cut accountability by identifying who is responsible for what.	
Save time	11. They save time by coordinating action and translating decisions into assignments.	
Support workers	12. They guide management to know how to support workers without over-supervising.	
Employee involvement	13. They provide good opportunity for employee involvement in the planning process itself.	
Ensure results	14. They ensure results by focusing all resources in the best possible way.	

Consumer Tech action plan

Here's what an initial sketch of the Consumer Tech action plan looked like:

Overall plan: Fully brief the board, develop a joint planning process, using a consultant to mediate the process					
Action	Responsible person				
1. Identify outside consultant	Chairman				
2. Investigate problems in manufacturing	Manufacturing Manager				
3. Estimate when quality will become reliable	Quality Manager				
4. Predict how long current stock will last	Finance Manager				
5. New feature introduction marketing plan	Marketing Manager				
6. Brief consultant	Chairman				
7. Fully brief the board	Chairman				
8. Set up joint planning process	Consultant				
9. Begin joint planning	Consultant				
10. Develop action plan for implementation	Chairman				

An action plan creates a practical programme to translate the decision or overall target into reality. This should resolve the problem and its side effects. The end result of Step 6 is a complete step-by-step road map of how to implement the decision.

Action planning tools

The following seven tools should help problem-solvers and decision-makers to generate a workable road map for implementing their decisions. Each will be briefly considered. The tools are:

1. Recovery
2. Brainstorming
3. Question and answer
4. Organising
5. Monitoring
6. Resource estimation
7. Contingency planning.

1. Recovery

You probably have a number of action items in your notes from previous steps. Don't waste these thoughts. After deleting those focused on other root causes or decision strategies, others should be valuable enough to transfer. Record any workable ideas on to the work sheet below.

ACTION ITEM WORK SHEET

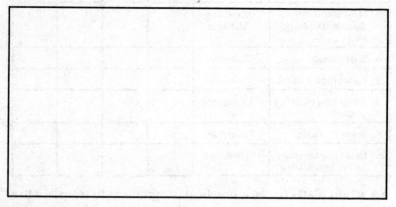

2. Brainstorming

Continue your creative thinking by brainstorming on the *Action item work sheet*. Questions which will serve as your target are:

What needs to be done to make this solution work?
Who should do what?
How do we get from here to there?
What is the most efficient budget and schedule?
How will we know if we're on or off track?
How will we follow up to ensure completion?

3. Question and answer

Use the *Action planning question checklist* to add to your list. Go through the questions one by one and when you feel each has been thoroughly answered, tick it off and move on to the next one. This comprehensive approach will help to ensure that all bases are covered.

ACTION PLANNING QUESTION CHECKLIST

1. What is the overall objective and ideal situation? _____
2. What is needed in order to get from here to there? _____
3. What actions need to be taken? _____
4. Who will be responsible for each action? _____
5. How long will each step take and when should it be done? _____
6. What is the best sequence of actions? _____
7. How can we be sure that earlier steps will be completed in time for later steps which depend on them? _____
8. What training is required to ensure that all staff have sufficient know-how to execute each step in the plan? _____
9. What standards do you want to set? _____
10. What level of volume or quality is desirable? _____
11. What resources are needed and how will we get them? _____
12. How will we measure results? _____
13. How will we follow up each step and who will do it? _____
14. What checkpoints and milestones should be established? _____
15. What are the vital make/break steps and how can we ensure that they succeed? _____
16. What could go wrong and how will we get round it? _____
17. Who will this plan effect and how will it affect them? _____
18. How can the plan be adjusted without jeopardising its results to ensure the best response and impact? _____
19. How will we communicate the plan to ensure support? _____
20. What response to change and other human factors are anticipated and how will they be overcome? _____

4. Organising

Use the *Action plan form* to put all your proposed actions together in an orderly fashion. The overall target box should be filled in first with the solution strategy you're trying to implement (chosen in Step 5). Then arrange the specific tasks from the *Action item work sheet* in sequence in the action column. Next, consider the staff available and assign who will be responsible for what on the form. Individual training and development are too often forgotten in Step 6. Be sure to include who needs to learn what to make the plan work.

ACTION PLAN FORM

Date:

Overall Target:					
Action	Responsible person	Performance standard	Monitoring technique	Completion deadline	Resources needed
1.					
2.					
3.					
4.					
5.					
6.					
7.					
8.					
9.					
10.					
11.					
12.					
13.					
14.					

5. Monitoring

The next column to complete on the *Action plan form* is for monitoring technique. Here you decide how well each function must be carried out and establish a *performance standard* (the third column). Measurable quotas, targets, goals or objectives are good choices. This provides a head start on establishing a monitoring system to track the plan's implementation.

Timing is another essential element of the monitoring process. Each item needs a firm *completion deadline*. Long or complex activities may benefit from one or several intermediate checkpoints as well.

Things never go exactly as planned. You need to establish a communication and follow-up system so that everyone involved stays informed and keeps the project on track. How will you check back with assigned staff, compare performance with the expected standards, and follow up to see that assignments will be completed on time?

The *Monitoring techniques checklist* suggests methods which can be used for each action item. Select the most appropriate, accurate, easiest and reliable method which will show both manager and performer how well things are progressing. The best monitoring is self-administered, while the boss and team are watching.

MONITORING TECHNIQUES CHECKLIST

1. Production count statistics _____
2. Quality control spot checks _____
3. Work sampling by management _____
4. Personal inspection of all work _____
5. MBWA (management by walking around) _____
6. Checkpoints on action plan _____
7. Reflective indicator statistics (measuring indirect consequences) _____
8. Trend analysis (typically using graphs) _____
9. Compliance reports _____

10. Regular activity reports   _____

11. Chase-up file   _____

12. One-to-one review meetings   _____

13. Group staff meetings   _____

14. Climate/attitude surveys and written questionnaires   _____

15. Customer/user interviews   _____

16. Checklist evaluation/audit   _____

17. Fitness report essay (comparing actual to ideal)   _____

18. Walk through/role play/dummy run procedure   _____

19. Budget controls   _____

20. Grapevine   _____

21. Gut feel   _____

6. Resource estimation

Time is a limited and easily expendable resource, especially without careful action planning, though cash is watched even more closely in well-run businesses. This is the best time to calculate logistics, budgets, and other hard resources. Include your estimates in the *Resources needed* column of the form.

7. Contingency planning

By this time anyone going to the trouble of developing an action plan will think it's near perfect. But what about a small dose of humility? To avoid human and job sacrifices to Murphy's Law, the best insurance is a little contingency planning. Obstacles to successful implementation can be obvious or hidden. Use the *Contingency planning work sheet* to think through what could go wrong, what you can do to avoid it, and if the worst comes to worst, how will you get out of the pickle.

CONTINGENCY PLANNING WORK SHEET

What could go wrong?	How could you prevent it from happening?	How will you fix it if it happens?

How to handle resistance to change

One contingency too often ignored is the all-important human factor. People who weren't involved in the PS/DM outline analysis may misunderstand the solution. Anticipate where you'll run into resistance to change and again decide how to prevent or combat it. The following chart should provide some helpful suggestions.

1. **Accept it**	People need stability and change destabilises. Expect resistance, fear and insecurity when people face the new and unfamiliar.
2. **Empathise**	Try to understand the reaction by studying another's point of view for a moment. If you see the personal and emotional impact change creates, you can handle it better.
3. **Know before you go**	Before you introduce change, find out what you're dealing with. Don't rush into the new until you are an expert on the old and current way of doing things. If necessary, wait until an auspicious time.
4. **Analyse the consequences**	Who will it affect? How? What might happen that you haven't considered? Consider all possible eventualities and adjust your proposal to maximise the desirable and minimise the undesirable consequences. (If you can't change what you want to, drop it.)
5. **Involve staff**	Ask others for input on the new plan, problems it creates, potential benefits, how best to implement it. By asking, discussing, accepting and group problem-solving, not only will the staff buy into the change, they'll improve on it and make it more workable.
6. **Give advance warning**	The sooner you announce that change is coming, the better. The longer the lead time, the less the shock, and the easier the emotional and intellectual adjustment.
7. **Beat the grapevine**	Manage the PR (public relations) of your idea effectively. If the idea leaks and the grapevine precedes your announcement, you've got an extra credibility gap to dig yourself out of.
8. **Present it positively**	Sell your idea to everyone affected in a way calculated to appeal broadly, and minimise shock, fear and hostility. Be prepared, composed, and constructive – not spur of the moment pig-headed.

9. **Ventilate resistance**	Sometimes people just need to ventilate the emotional shock of the unexpected and untried without any response from the boss. Letting them blow off steam in a group planning session or even one-to-one first can clear the air for rational thought.
10. **Stress benefits**	Initially, emphasise the needs and problems of others and how the change will help them, not you. If it's for them, it's more likely to be viewed as desirable and worth the trouble. You can even offer appropriate rewards for swift, smooth cooperation.
11. **Explain the purpose**	If people can see why you want to go to all this trouble, they may join the effort. Ideally, the team will agree, so start your presentation in terms of the organisational problem you want to solve or the improvement to be accomplished.
12. **Reassure them**	An immediate promise from the boss that no one will lose their job, pay, or future will help. Anticipate specific individual fears and assure all that the worst won't happen, confidently and realistically.
13. **Stress growth**	Many people want to get ahead. Change creates opportunities. If you reinforce new approaches by highlighting possible chances for advancement and development, you can entice the ambitious ones over to your side.
14. **Include training**	In both your plans and announcements, be sure to include enough re-education and on-the-job training to make the transition smooth. People want to do a quality job, so prevent the fear of failure by promising and conducting supportive training.
15. **Change gradually**	Don't expect major readjustment overnight. Plan for step-by-step change, fast enough to keep the energy up but slow enough so each step can be taken smoothly and certainly.
16. **Recognise your supporters**	Each step of the way acknowledge constructive advice and willing cooperation. A sincere and loud 'Thank you' afterwards will do an awful lot for improving the climate for change next time.

A final action plan test

After constructing an action plan but before giving the go-ahead, evaluate it using the *Action plan test*. By testing it against the 13 criteria, you'll get a good sense of its relative effectiveness and completeness. The best action planners religiously play devil's advocate with their draft work, and adjust it wherever necessary until it has the highest chance of coming off without a hitch.

ACTION PLAN TEST

Criteria

Does your action plan identify . . .	Yes	No
1. Specific actions	☐	☐
2. Clear responsibilities	☐	☐
3. Realistic deadlines	☐	☐
4. Clear-cut targets (performance standards and production quotas	☐	☐
5. A coordinated sequence of actions	☐	☐
6. A realistic and workable system	☐	☐
7. Checkpoints for routine follow-up	☐	☐
8. Reliable measurement of results	☐	☐
9. Needed personal development	☐	☐
10. Correctly emphasised priorities	☐	☐
11. Feasible contingency plans (for risky actions or things that might go wrong)	☐	☐
12. Agreements workable for all involved	☐	☐
13. A good chance of achieving the ideal scene	☐	☐

CHAPTER 10
Summary

Evaluation of your objectives

After working through the problem-solving and decision-making processes presented here, evaluate your personal progress. On a scale of 1 to 10 (10 = high) rate how well you've achieved each of the 13 objectives of this system:

Outline   1. Understand the systematic rational problem-solving outline. _____

Techniques   2. Know how to use the various analytical techniques for each phase. _____

Communication   3. Recognise the vital role communication plays at each step. _____

Questions   4. Know what questions to use in order to stimulate communication at each phase. _____

Anatomy   5. Understand the anatomy of problems and why they persist. _____

Prevent stress   6. Understand how to confront problems to prevent future stress. _____

Cause and effect 7. Know how to distinguish between problem causes and effects. _____

Label   8. Know how to label a problem to facilitate discussion and analysis. _____

Root cause   9. Know how to find a problem's
                       root cause.   _____

Solutions   10. Know why it's important and
                       how to brainstorm optional
                       solutions.   _____

Decisions   11. Know how to evaluate optional
                       solutions to decide on the most
                       workable strategy.   _____

Action plans   12. Understand the importance of
                       action-planning to implement
                       the chosen solution.   _____

Application   13. Know how to use the resource
                       materials to apply the system
                       to real-life problems as they
                       occur in the future.   _____

Personal summary

Answer the following questions to wrap things up and set your sights on the future:

List the key points of this book that you found most valuable:

Which of your personal expectations have been achieved?

Now that you know the PS/DM outline, what part of the systematic process have you been applying correctly?

What mistakes have you inadvertently been making in dealing with problems and solutions?

What do you plan to do to improve your problem-solving and decision-making skills?

How do you plan to apply what you've learned?

Further Reading from Kogan Page

Creative Thinking in Business: A Practical Guide, Carol Kinsey Goman

Effective Meeting Skills: How to Make Meetings More Productive, Marion E Haynes

Effective Performance Appraisals, Robert B Maddux

Effective Presentation Skills, Steve Mandel

The Fifty-Minute Supervisor: A Guide for the Newly Promoted, Elwood N Chapman

How to Communicate Effectively, Bert Decker

How to Develop a Positive Attitude, Elwood N Chapman

How to Make Meetings Work, Malcolm Peel

How to Motivate People, Twyla Dell

Improving Relations at Work, Elwood N Chapman

Leadership Skills for Women, Marilyn Manning and Patricia Haddock

Make Every Minute Count: How to Manage Your Time Effectively, Marion E Haynes

Managing Disagreement Constructively, Herbert S Kindler

Managing Organisational Change, Cynthia D Scott and Dennis T Jaffe

Profits from Improved Productivity, Fiona Halse and John Humphrey

Project Management, Marion E Haynes

Quality at Work, Diane Bone and Rick Griggs

Successful Negotiation, Robert B Maddux

Team Building: An Exercise in Leadership, Robert B Maddux